Contents

Introduction

Who Was Shakespeare?

William Shakespeare is probably the most famous playwright in the world. He was born in 1564 in Stratford-upon-Avon, and four hundred years after his death his plays are still being performed all over the world in almost every language you can think of. Although he came from a fairly ordinary family and didn't even go to university, he wrote thirty-eight plays with exciting plots and new, dramatic language.

Most of his plays were performed at the Globe, one of the very first theatres in London. Some were also performed for Queen Elizabeth I herself at court. Because he was also an actor and probably appeared in some of his own plays, Shakespeare knew what audiences liked. He became one of the most popular playwrights of his day and, by the time he died in 1616, he was a wealthy man.

Health and Disease

Kathy Elgin

Illustrated by Adam Hook

CHERRYTREE BOOKS

First published in paperback in 2009

Published in Great Britain by Cherrytree
Books, part of the Evans Publishing Group.
2a Portman Mansions,
Chiltern Street
London W1U 6NR

Produced for Evans Brothers by
Bailey Publishing Associates Ltd
11a Woodlands
Hove BN3 6TJ

Editor: Alex Woolf
Designer: Simon Borrough
Artwork: Adam Hook
Picture research: Glass Onion Pictures

British Library Cataloguing in Publication Data
Elgin, Kathy, 1948
   Health and disease - (Shakespeare's world)
   1. Shakespeare, William, 1564-1616 -
   Themes, motives - Juvenile literature
   2. Health - History - 16th century -
   Juvenile literature
   3. Health - History - 17th century -
   Juvenile literature
   4. Public Health - England - History -
   16th century - Juvenile literature
   5. Public Health - England - History -
   17th century - Juvenile literature
   6. Diseases - England - History - 16th
   century - Juvenile literature
   7. Diseases - England - History - 17th
   century - Juvenile literature
   8. Great Britain - History - Elizabeth,
   1558-1603 - Juvenile literature
   I. Title
   614. 4'0942'09031

ISBN 978 1 842345382

Printed and bound in China

Titles in this series:
Daily Life
Crime and Punishment
Health and Disease
Theatre and Entertainment

Cover background: A detail from *The Triumph of
Death* by Pieter Bruegel the Elder (1525–1569).

Picture Acknowledgements:
The publishers would like to thank the
following for permission to reproduce their
pictures:
Adam Hart-Davis: 6; Art Archive: cover
(background), cover (portrait) and 4, 8 (Museo
della Civilta Romana, Rome), 11 (Museo del
Prado, Madrid), 14, 15 (Museo Correr, Venice
/ Dagli Orti [A]); Bridgeman Art Library: 9
(Mauritshuis, the Hague), 10 (Stapleton
Collection), 13t, 13b (Kunsthistorisches
Museum, Vienna), 17t, 17b (Glasgow University
Library, Scotland), 19, 21 (Chelsea Physic
Garden, London), 22 (Linnean Society,
London), 25 (Musée de l'Hotel Sandelin,
Saint-Omer / Lauros / Giraudon), 27b
(Galleria dell' Accademia, Florence), 28
(Bibliotheque de l'Institut d'Ophtalmologie,
Paris), 29; Topham: 7 (Corporation of
London), 18 (Fotomas), 20 (Science Museum,
London), 23 (John Maier, Jr. / The Image
Works), 24, 27t (Topfoto / Fotomas).

Health and Disease in Shakespeare's Time

Shakespeare lived in a period when new scientific knowledge had begun to replace the old superstitions which people had believed for a thousand years. At the same time, many of the poor and uneducated still believed in magic. Many still thought that illnesses and outbreaks of plague were a punishment from God for their wicked behaviour.

A lot of the health problems were in fact caused, or made worse, by poor food, bad housing and a lack of hygiene. Doctors suspected some of this, but could not prove it. They did not yet have microscopes powerful enough to show them bacteria. They did not really understand the scientific reason for illnesses, but had to treat people according to the old theories in their textbooks. Some of these were actually quite dangerous.

Shakespeare talks a great deal about doctors and medicine in his plays. This is probably because his son-in-law, John Hall, was a doctor in Stratford. Shakespeare must have heard a lot about illness and remedies from him. He also uses images from medical sources, showing us how widely understood these things were at that time.

Several doctors appear in his plays. In *King Lear* and *Macbeth* they are kind men who care for their patients and are respected in society. Dr Pinch in *The Comedy of Errors*, however, is a fake, while Cerimon in *Pericles* has the mystical powers of a magician. This shows us how doctors and medicine were thought of in Shakespeare's day.

Health and Hygiene

Poor diet, bad housing and lack of hygiene were worst among the poor in London. People did not bath much, and fleas and lice were common. Narrow London streets, made narrower by overhanging upper storeys, shut out sunlight and fresh air. A gutter down the middle of the street overflowed with dirty water and sewage. From here the waste flowed into ditches and then straight into the Thames. Contaminated water brought killer diseases like typhoid fever, typhus, cholera and dysentery.

> Art thou so bare and full of wretchedness,
> And fear'st to die? famine is in thy cheeks,
> Need and oppression starveth in thy eyes,
> Contempt and beggary hangs upon thy back.
> ROMEO AND JULIET, ACT 5, SCENE 1

contempt: disgrace
beggary: poverty

Romeo is speaking to an apothecary who is so poor and hungry that he is prepared to break the law and sell Romeo poison. Many people existed on the edge of starvation. Food production could hardly keep up with the fast-growing population. If the grain harvest failed, there was famine. This happened several times in the mid-sixteenth century. At the best of times there was not much variety in the diet. With very little fresh meat or fresh fruit and vegetables, people suffered from scurvy, caused by lack of vitamins.

The castle garderobe was usually in the corner of a turret room and not very private. Instead of toilet paper, moss or leaves were used.

> *Is Brutus sick,*
> *And will he steal out of his wholesome bed,*
> *To dare the vile contagion of the night?*
> JULIUS CAESAR, ACT 2, SCENE 1

dare: confront

These lines are spoken by Brutus's wife and, like many Elizabethans, she thought that illnesses were caused by some sort of infectious vapour in the air. This was believed to be especially dangerous in the damp night air, in fog or in marshy places. In fact, the infection probably came from the toilet. The poor emptied chamber pots or buckets into cesspits near the house.

Even in castles, the "garderobe" was just a seat suspended over a shaft leading down to the moat or a pit which was cleaned out once a year.

Professional rat-catchers were employed to keep down the vermin which fed on the rubbish in the streets.

Housewives threw waste and rubbish out of the window, crying "gardy-loo" (from the French for "mind the water").

Theories about Health

Medical knowledge was slowly beginning to replace the old beliefs. For centuries scholars had followed the teachings of the ancient Greeks. They believed that bodies were made up of fluids governed by four "humours" – choler, blood, phlegm and melancholy. These corresponded to the natural elements of fire, water, air and earth. Illness was caused when one humour became out of proportion to the others, and treatment consisted of correcting the balance. A great physician called Galen, working in Rome around 170 CE, developed these theories further. But by Shakespeare's time the physician Vesalius had begun to transform medical knowledge completely by questioning all previous theories.

A bust of the physician Galen.

> *Does not our life consist of the four elements?*
> TWELFTH NIGHT, ACT 2, SCENE 3

Most Elizabethan doctors still used Galen's works as their main reference book when diagnosing illness.

We can't tell whether Sir Toby here really still believes in the elements. These theories lingered on among the poor, but the way Shakespeare refers to them suggests that educated people thought they were already out of date. In *Coriolanus* there is a long fable about parts of the body rebelling against the stomach for greedily hoarding food. This suggests that people knew about the digestive system and blood, although they did not yet understand circulation.

> *What says the doctor to my water?*
>
> *He said, sir, the water itself was a good healthy water; but, for the party that owed it, he might have moe diseases than he knew for.*
>
> HENRY IV, PART 2, ACT 1, SCENE 2

water: urine
owed: owned
moe: more

Elizabethan medicine was mostly based on observation. Studying the urine was the first step in diagnosis. This was where any imbalance of the humours would be revealed. Urine samples are still the basis of much modern diagnosis, although of course doctors don't believe in humours any more. Elizabethans were also correct in thinking that one of the best remedies was sleep. Macbeth's wife, for example, is right when she tells him that sleep is the best thing to calm his nerves after he has committed murder.

Vesalius' drawings showed, for the first time, the position and workings of the muscles and organs in the human body.

UNDECIMA
MUSCULO-
RVM TA-
BVLA.

Common Complaints

Some of Shakespeare's characters suffer from illnesses and complaints that we can recognise, even if they have different names for them. Shakespeare records the symptoms and treatment of falling sickness (epilepsy), from which both Othello and Julius Caesar suffer. Toby Belch has indigestion and Falstaff has gout, both brought on by drinking too much. People had poor eyesight from too much reading by candlelight, but few could afford spectacles. The writer William Harrison even thought that modern luxuries were making people soft. They caught more rheums (colds) in their fine new houses, which were draughty and had smoky chimneys.

As we can see in this sugar mill, sugar was sold in large "loaves" from which bits were chipped off as required.

> *There was never yet philosopher*
> *That could endure the toothache patiently.*
> MUCH ADO ABOUT NOTHING,
> ACT 5, SCENE 1

Tooth decay was one of the few ailments that mainly affected the rich. This was because they ate far too much sugar, which the poor could not afford. As a visiting ambassador noted, even Queen Elizabeth's teeth were quite black. Rubbing the teeth with ashes of rosemary leaves or ground alabaster helped to prevent decay. A more desperate remedy was to have them scraped and bleached with nitric acid. After a few treatments the teeth fell out or had to be pulled by the barber — without anaesthetic.

And purge it to a sound and pristine health, I would applaud thee to the very echo.

Not surprisingly, many people suffered toothache rather than go to a barber, or tooth-puller.

> *If thou couldst, doctor, cast*
> *The water of my land, find her disease,*
> *And purge it to a sound and pristine health,*
> *I would applaud thee to the very echo.*
>
> MACBETH, ACT 5, SCENE 3

Once a problem had been identified through inspecting the urine ("casting the water"), the basic treatment was purging. This was done by repeatedly making the patient sick, starving him or giving an enema. This was to supposed to flush the evil out of the system and level the balance of the humours. An alternative was bleeding, to rid the body of "bad" blood. Bleeding often left patients so weak that they were unable to recover.

Bleeding was done by cutting into a vein and letting the blood drip.

Surviving Birth and Childhood

Childbirth was an experience that all women feared. Many of them died along with their babies, either from complications or loss of blood. The tight-fitting clothing that women wore, even when pregnant, often harmed both mother and foetus. Doctors were rarely involved in childbirth, and if anything went wrong there was little that could be done. Babies who reached their first birthday stood a reasonable chance of survival, but this did not mean they were healthy. Childhood ailments like rickets, caused by lack of vitamins, left many with crooked legs. Babies were wrapped in tight swaddling clothes for their first year, sometimes preventing their limbs from growing properly.

A terrible childbed hast thou had, my dear;
No light, no fire: th'unfriendly elements
Forgot thee utterly.
PERICLES, PRINCE OF TYRE,
ACT 3, SCENE 1

childbed: labour, experience of giving birth

Pericles's wife Thaisa dies after giving birth at sea during a storm. Most women had their babies at home. In better-off households this was quite a ritual. Having a baby was more of a social event than a medical process. Pregnant women moved into a specially prepared room for the month-long "lying-in". They were attended by female friends and relatives or sometimes by a midwife. After the birth they stayed in bed for three days and did not take up normal life for several weeks.

Toddlers were put into mini-versions of adult clothes, which were almost as restricting as their swaddling.

they that went on crutches ere he was born desire

> *... it is a gallant child; one that, indeed, physics the subject, makes old hearts fresh: they that went on crutches ere he was born desire yet their life to see him a man.*
>
> THE WINTER'S TALE,
> ACT 1, SCENE 1

physics: does good

Female relatives who gathered to help with an expected birth often stayed on for several weeks.

Sadly, little Prince Mamillius, referred to here, later dies. Many families had their hopes disappointed in this way. Three out of every twenty babies died in their first year, and one in twenty died before they were four. Shakespeare's own son Hamnet died at eleven. Most babies died from sickness caught from contaminated water. Others died from malnutrition, or from accidents such as falling into open fires.

Jane Seymour, third wife of Henry VIII, died shortly after giving birth to their son Edward, who died himself aged just sixteen.

13

Plague

Plague had been common in England since medieval times. It was the disease people feared most. It spread rapidly in the overcrowded cities, wiping out whole communities at a time. People thought the infection was transmitted through the air, so they carried scented handkerchiefs or pomanders of sweet herbs to ward it off. In fact it was spread by fleas which picked up the infection from diseased rats. When plague struck, theatres were closed and people were forbidden to gather in large groups.

> *... the searchers of the town,*
> *Suspecting that we both were in a house*
> *Where the infectious pestilence did reign,*
> *Sealed up the doors, and would not let us forth.*
> ROMEO AND JULIET, ACT 5, SCENE 2

pestilence: plague

A list of deaths and burials was printed every week during the plague years in London, illustrated by this grim woodcut.

When plague broke out, the rich packed up and left the city for their country houses. They remained there until the outbreak was over. The poor had to stay put. If they became infected they were locked up in their houses, the healthy and the dying together. Bodies were collected and buried in plague pits. After a particularly bad outbreak, in London in 1593, a special isolation hospital, or pest-house, was built to house victims.

For the Lord's tokens in you do I see.

> They are infected, in their hearts it lies;
> They have the plague, and caught it of your eyes:
> These lords are visited; you are not free,
> For the Lord's tokens in you do I see.
>
> LOVE'S LABOUR'S LOST, ACT 5, SCENE 2

of: from
visited: infected
tokens: signs

Symptoms of the plague were buboes, or swellings, in the armpit and groin. These were known as "tokens", and those who had them had been "visited", as in this quote. People believed plague was a punishment from God for their sins. The only treatment was rubbing the swellings with salt, or burning them with red-hot irons. Plague was so common that everybody would understand immediately when Shakespeare used imagery like this.

Plague victims discovered buboes about three days after being infected, and eight out of ten died within the week.

The "beak" of this plague-mask is stuffed with cotton soaked in herbal oils to prevent the doctor breathing in the infection.

They have the plague, and caught it of your eyes: These lords are visited; you are not free,

15

Doctors

There were many different kinds of doctor. Physicians had the highest status. They had to have a university degree, followed by many years of medical study, probably in France or Italy. They studied anatomy and probably dissected human corpses. Only a physician was allowed to prescribe physic (medicine). Physicians regarded themselves as scholars and often did not actually examine their patients. They diagnosed complaints and decided on treatment largely with the help of textbooks. Most of the practical treatment was done by surgeons. They were not as learned as physicians, but were properly trained and licensed by the Company of Barber-Surgeons. The third class of medical practitioner was the apothecary, who made up and dispensed remedies.

For the love of God, a surgeon! Send one presently to Sir Toby…. He has broke my head across, and has given Sir Toby a bloody coxcomb too.

TWELFTH NIGHT, ACT 5, SCENE 1

coxcomb: head

A physician, wearing the formal robes and hat of his profession, studies a flask of his patient's urine.

Surgeons, or barber-surgeons, mostly dealt with everyday accidents and illnesses. They set broken bones, healed wounds and performed minor surgery such as cutting veins to let out "bad" blood. They also performed operations, although these were rare in Shakespeare's day. They did not have such a wide knowledge of general medicine as physicians and were not allowed to prescribe medicines. They also did dental work and everyday jobs like cutting hair and shaving.

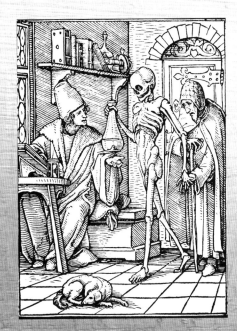

This unhappy patient is being led to the doctor by a skeleton, Death, also carrying a urine flask.

'Tis known I ever
Have studied physic, through which secret art,
... I have,
Together with my practice, made familiar
To me and to my aid the blest infusions
That dwells in vegetives, in metals, stones ...

PERICLES, ACT 3, SCENE 2

physic: medicine
infusions: natural properties
vegetives: plants

Although Cerimon here has studied as a physician, he also dabbles in alchemy, a kind of magic. Many people believed in the mystical healing effect of stones and metals as well as herbs. Although at the time they thought of this as magic, it was the beginning of the science of chemistry. Eventually it produced the powerful drugs we use today.

Although dissection was vital to the advance of medical knowledge, the church did not approve of it, so classes like this were rare.

17

Non-Professional Healers

Even if people could afford to consult a doctor, there simply were not enough of them to go round. A law of 1542 allowed non-professionals to practise, as long as they did not charge a fee. Apothecaries offered free advice, but made their living by selling herbal remedies. In country districts, people had to cure themselves. Married women were responsible for the health of their families. Much of their medical knowledge was passed down from mother to daughter, either in letters and family notebooks or – since many could not read – by word of mouth.

Apothecaries' shops like this one were kept busy making up cheap remedies for people who could not afford to see a doctor.

Trust not the physician;
His antidotes are poison,
and he slays
More than you rob.
TIMON OF ATHENS,
ACT 4, SCENE 3

Professional doctors had the unfair reputation of killing more patients than they cured. Because of the expense, people often only consulted them when they were already too ill to be cured. By this time they had probably dosed themselves with home remedies. As the doctor's medicine was not much better than these, it is not surprising that patients failed to recover.

whereof The king is rendered lost.

There is a remedy, approved,

> There is a remedy, approved, set down.
> To cure the desperate languishings whereof
> The king is rendered lost.
> ALL'S WELL THAT ENDS WELL, ACT 1, SCENE 3

languishings: wasting disease
rendered: declared

Helena, speaking here, is the daughter of a famous physician. Although she is unqualified, she uses his remedies to cure the king of a mysterious illness. It was impossible for women to qualify as doctors because they were not allowed to go to university. Many, however, practised unofficially, especially as midwives. They were known as wise women. Some became famous, like Grace Mildmay (1552–1620), who learned medicine from a poor relation, and Lady Margaret Hoby, who kept a diary from 1599 to 1605. She wrote about the health of her family and noted down her herbal remedies. There were dangers, though. Many wise women were burned as witches when their remedies failed to work.

Many unwary patients found themselves at the mercy of "quacks" – fraudulent doctors with useless remedies.

Women had to cope with serious illness in the family, as well as everyday accidents.

19

Cures and Remedies

Most remedies treated the symptoms of illness rather than the cause. They were based on the theory of opposites: someone who had a fever and felt hot was given medicine made from a "cold" plant like lettuce to cool them down. Painful areas had to be treated with something of a similar appearance. Ivory was used to cure toothache, because ivory and teeth looked much the same. Often they used the right treatment although their reasoning was wrong. For example, watercress was a good remedy, not because it was "cold and wet" but because it contains a lot of vitamin C.

The second property of your excellent sherris is the warming of the blood, which before, cold and set-tled, left the liver white and pale.

HENRY IV PART 2, ACT 4, SCENE 3

sherris: sherry

Apothecaries kept their drugs in fine Italian earthenware jars called albarelli. Next to this is the title page of Gerard's famous Herbal (see page 22).

Shakespeare's fat hero Falstaff, who knows all about the theory of humours, thinks that a bottle of sherry is the best remedy. By warming up the blood it revives the different parts of the body and makes men brave. By drying out the damp "vapours" in the brain it makes them clever and witty. Of course, this is just Falstaff's excuse for drinking too much, but the reasons he gives would have made good sense to Shakespeare's audiences.

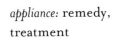

appliance: remedy, treatment

... Diseases desperate grown
By desperate appliance are relieved,
Or not at all.

HAMLET, ACT 4, SCENE 3

An apothecary's apprentice grinds drugs using a pestle and mortar.

This lovely book shows two doctors making accurate botanical drawings for a textbook.

Most remedies were fairly harmless. Some, however, were quite extreme. Regular bleeding, vomiting and the use of laxatives made patients very weak. Swellings or sores were treated with poultices, or plasters smeared with ointment. These were safe for use on the skin, but they contained dozens of different ingredients, some of which proved deadly if they got into the body through an open wound. Many people suspected that King James I was poisoned by a plaster prescribed as a cure during his final illness.

Herbs and Herbals

Every house had a herb garden growing plants for medical use as well as for cooking. Housewives knew enough about herbs to make their own remedies. Those who needed advice could buy books like *The English Housewife*, *The Castle of Health* or *The Accomplished Lady's Delight*. These also gave beauty tips, such as how to distil special herbal waters to keep hands soft, skin white and hair blonde. Other books, which identified plants, were known as herbals. The most famous is John Gerard's, published in 1594. It has beautiful illustrations of each plant and notes on how to use the different parts.

> *O, mickle is the powerful grace, that lies*
> *In plants, herbs, stones, and their true qualities.*
> ROMEO AND JULIET, ACT 2, SCENE 3

mickle: great
grace: virtue, good thing

Many of the plant remedies were already ancient. Comfrey, sometimes called knitbone, was for healing broken bones. Marigold flowers were good for cuts and sores, and liquorice and senna were used as laxatives to purge the system. Sage was used as an antiseptic, and lemon balm treated fevers. The Chelsea Physic Garden, established fifty years after Shakespeare's death, still grows all these medicinal plants.

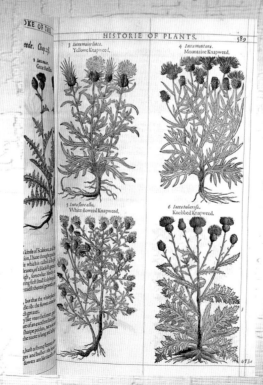

Gerard's Herbal illustrated many plants commonly found growing wild, like this knapweed, a kind of thistle.

22

> Within the infant rind of this weak flower
> Poison hath residence, and medicine power:
> For this, being smelt, with that part cheers each part;
> Being tasted, slays all senses with the heart.
>
> ROMEO AND JULIET, ACT 2, SCENE 3

infant rind: unripe peel

The foxglove grows wild everywhere but could prove a deadly plant.

As the herbalist Friar Laurence tells us here, each part of a plant had a different use. Apothecaries — and housewives — had to know which to use. Women used juice from the foxglove to make their eyes look bigger, and it was also used to treat heart complaints. Taken in large doses, though, it could kill. Many Elizabethan court scandals involved poisoning with plant juices. Queen Elizabeth's own doctor was executed for trying to poison her.

Many of the old herbal remedies have been rediscovered and are being prescribed today.

Madness

The Elizabethans were fascinated by madness, but were not at all sympathetic to sufferers. They did not think of insanity as an illness, and doctors hardly bothered to treat it. Many believed it was caused by the moon, or that people were possessed by devils. If a priest could not rid them of the devils, people were simply locked up for the rest of their lives. The first institution for the insane was Bethlehem Hospital, or Bedlam, in London. Even here, people were treated more like prisoners than patients. Some were cared for at home, if they were not too violent. Any found roaming the countryside were called bedlam beggars.

King Lear began to lose his wits after he was treated cruelly by his daughters and turned out of the house.

> *Love is merely a madness, and, I tell you, deserves as well a dark house and a whip as madmen do.*
> AS YOU LIKE IT, ACT 3, SCENE 2

It was thought that punishment might bring madmen to their senses. As well as being locked up in the dark, they were often beaten by the warders. Shakespeare mentions this in both *The Comedy of Errors* and *Twelfth Night*, where a cruel trick is played on someone. Shakespeare mentions madness over 250 times in his plays. Several characters, like King Lear and Ophelia, really do go mad. Hamlet only pretends to be mad, but behaves very convincingly.

deserves as well a dark

> *Canst thou not minister to a mind diseas'd,*
> *Pluck from the memory a rooted sorrow*
> MACBETH, ACT 5, SCENE 3

minister: take care of, treat

Macbeth and his wife have both done terrible things in the past. Now guilt has made them both mad. Madmen appeared very frequently in Elizabethan plays, but most writers used them as comic characters or rather sinister figures. Shakespeare tried to show why they were troubled and what had led them to this sad state. He realized that people were often tormented by things they could not forget or forgive. He was far ahead of his time in this attitude.

Violent madmen were kept chained to the wall like prisoners.

Some doctors believed that the "mad" part could be cut out of a patient, like removing teeth.

Hospitals

Medieval hospitals were attached to monasteries and were run by monks and nuns. They were skilled herbalists who cared for the sick but also took in the poor and homeless. In the 1530s, however, Henry VIII closed down the monasteries. The old monastery-hospitals were given new charters, and four royal hospitals were created in London.

Elizabethan hospitals were more like a hospice, where people went for care rather than for operations or specialist treatment. They still cared for children and the poor, although they were no longer connected to the Church.

> ... *well, befall what will befall,*
> *I'll jest a twelvemonth in an hospital.*
> LOVE'S LABOUR'S LOST, ACT 5,
> SCENE 2

befall: happen
twelvemonth: year

This character is being made to visit the sick as a way of making him more grown-up and responsible. Visiting the sick was regarded as a charitable act. Conditions in hospital were not always good, but they were clean, and more hygienic than most people's homes. Remedies were provided but, whenever possible, the patient's family had to bring in food and clothing, as they did with people in prison.

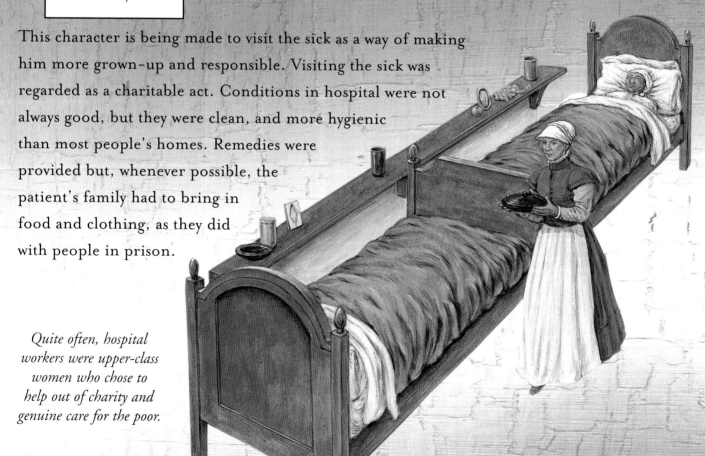

Quite often, hospital workers were upper-class women who chose to help out of charity and genuine care for the poor.

26

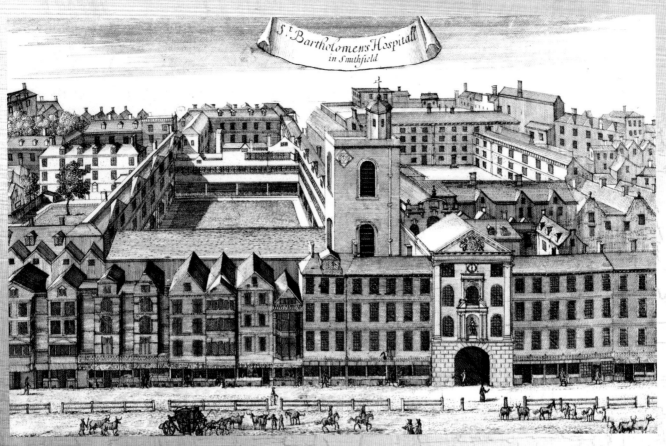

St Bartholomews Hospitall in Smithfield

St Bartholomew's was one of the royal hospitals created by Henry VIII and Edward VI.

> *News have I that my Nell is dead i' th' spital*
> *Of malady of France.*
>
> HENRY V, ACT 5, SCENE 1

spital: hospital
malady: illness

People were usually sent to a hospital to keep them away from society. Temporary hospitals were set up whenever there was an outbreak of a major disease. Most towns had a pest-house on the outskirts where plague victims were kept. A lazar house was a similar institution for the care of lepers. Leprosy had been brought to England by the crusaders in about the thirteenth century. By Shakespeare's time it was rare, but people were very afraid of it because there was no known cure. Sufferers simply had to be isolated.

The architecture shows that the Hospital of St Matthew here was once part of a monastery.

...well, befall what will befall, I'll jest a twelvemonth in an hospital.

27

Wounds and Operations

Very few operations were performed. There were no anaesthetics, and surgeons could only make people drowsy with alcohol or opium. Patients were conscious throughout and often died from shock. Infection was another problem, as there was no way of sterilizing instruments. In wartime, though, surgery was essential. Battlefield operations were quick and agonizing. Injured limbs became infected with gangrene and had to be amputated. More men died from surgery or from the loss of blood than from the original injury. Many who survived the operation died slowly and in great pain from infections.

This is said to be an operation to remove cataracts from the eyes, a delicate operation even by today's standards.

> *I have some wounds upon me....*
>
> *... Well might they fester 'gainst ingratitude,*
> *And tent themselves with death.*
>
> CORIOLANUS, ACT 1, SCENE 9

The great hero Martius has twenty-seven wounds on his body. They are regarded as proof of his bravery. Infection and festering of wounds was a constant problem. "Tenting" meant probing with a cotton pad to cleanse the wound. At sea, the barber-surgeon had to operate while the ship was tossing about. Sailors stood ready to swill the blood off the table ready for the next patient. Amazingly, many sailors survived and even had wooden legs fitted to their stumps.

> Then will he strip his sleeve and show his scars,
> And say, "These wounds I had on Crispin's day."
> HENRY V, ACT 4, SCENE 3

Crispin: St Crispin

Until the mid-sixteenth century, wounds were treated with boiling oil or red-hot irons. This was terribly painful and left scars. One night in 1536, after a battle, a French army surgeon called Ambroise Paré ran out of oil. All he could do was to clean and dress the wounds. He expected his patients to die, but instead they recovered more quickly and had fewer scars. This proved a great advance in medical care.

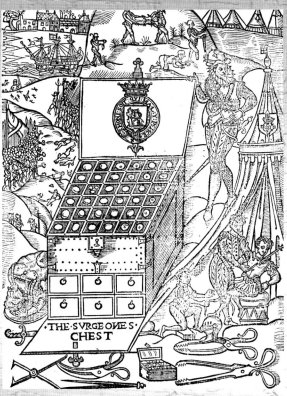

THE SVRGEONES CHEST

Left: The surgeon's medicine chest on Henry VIII's warship, the Mary Rose, which sank in 1545. When the chest was recovered over 400 years later, it still contained the remains of ointments.

Right: Wounded sailors often ended their lives as beggars.

Well might they fester 'gainst ingratitude, And tent themselves with death.

29

Timeline

1533	Princess Elizabeth, daughter of King Henry VIII, is born.
1536	Ambroise Paré discovers new ways of treating wounds.
1543	Publication of Vesalius' *On the Structure of the Human Body* in Latin
1546	St Bartholomew's hospital is reopened by royal charter after public petitions.
1552	St Thomas's hospital is reopened by royal charter.
1558	Elizabeth becomes Queen.
1563	Plague, spreading from Europe, kills 20,000 people in London.
1564	Shakespeare is born.
1565	Tobacco is first introduced to England, causing ill-health through smoking.
1567	Paracelsus's work on mental health is published, twenty-five years after his death.
1577–80	Sir Francis Drake sails round the world. Sailors bring back new diseases as well as new plants for medical use.
1580	New building in London is forbidden in an attempt to prevent unhealthy overcrowding.
1588	Defeat of the Spanish Armada: England is saved from invasion.
1594	Poor grain harvests lead to famine. Gerard's great *Herbal* is published.
1596	Shakespeare's son Hamnet dies, aged eleven.
1600	The population of England and Ireland reaches five and a half million.
1601	Poor Laws compel each parish to provide shelter for the poor and sick.
1603	Death of Queen Elizabeth in her seventieth year.
1607	Dr John Hall, Shakespeare's son-in-law, starts his medical practice in Stratford.
1612	The height of the witchcraft trials. Many "wise women" are burned to death.
1613	The cutting of the New River brings a cleaner water supply to London.
1615	*The English Housewife*, cookery book and general household manual, is published.
1616	Shakespeare dies of a fever, perhaps after a drinking party with Ben Jonson.
1628	William Harvey discovers how blood circulates in the body.

Glossary

Difficult Shakespearean words appear alongside each quotation. This glossary explains words used in the main text.

alabaster	A white rock.
alchemy	An early form of chemistry mixed with magic.
amputate	Cut off.
anaesthetic	A drug to put someone to sleep.
anatomy	The study of the physical structure of the body.
antiseptic	Disinfectant, destroying germs.
apothecary	A person who prepares drugs and remedies.
bacteria	Germs which cause disease.
bleeding	A medieval treatment involving cutting a vein to draw out "infected" blood. Also known as bloodletting.
cesspit	A hole for depositing sewage.
charter	Document from the monarch confirming the establishment of an organization.
cholera	A stomach infection involving diarrhoea.
crusaders	Those who fought in religious wars between the eleventh and thirteenth centuries CE.
diagnosis	Identification of an illness.
dispense	Mix and sell drugs.

Further

Information

dissect	Cut open a body in order to study its structure.
distil	Extract the essence.
dysentery	An infection of the intestines.
enema	A treatment to clean out the bowels.
epilepsy	A nervous complaint producing fits.
festering	Rotting, or oozing an infected discharge.
foetus	An unborn child.
gangrene	The decay of body tissue.
garderobe	A toilet.
gout	A painful swelling of the joints.
hospice	A home caring for the terminally ill.
humour	Bodily fluid.
hygiene	Cleanliness.
imbalance	Lack of balance.
laxative	Something to make you go to the toilet.
lazar	A leper.
leprosy	A disease causing disfigurement and loss of body parts.
lice	Bloodsucking insects (plural of "louse").
microscope	An instrument for magnifying.
mystical	Mysterious, supernatural.
opium	A drug made from poppy seeds.
phlegm	A slimy liquid made in the lungs.
pomander	Perforated ball containing sweet-smelling herbs.
poultice	A cloth soaked in medicine.
purge	Flush out of the system.
rheum	A cold.
rickets	A disease that makes the bones become soft, causing bow-legs.
scurvy	A disease which makes people anaemic and causes bleeding of the gums and skin.
sewage	Bodily waste.
sterilizing	Disinfect or make free of germs.
swaddling	Strips of cloth.
symptoms	Signs of an illness.
typhoid	A disease with high fever, a rash and stomach pain.
typhus	A disease with fever, spots and headache.
vapour	Moisture in the air.
warder	An officer in charge of prisoners.

Further Reading

Look Inside: a Tudor Medicine Chest by Brian Moses (Hodder Wayland, 1999)
You Wouldn't Want to be Ill in Tudor Times by Kathryn Senior (Hodder Wayland, 2002)
The History Detective Investigates: Tudor Medicine by Richard Tames (Hodder Wayland, 2002)

Eyewitness: Shakespeare by Peter Chrisp (Dorling Kindersley, 2002)
The Illustrated World of the Tudors by Peter Chrisp (Hodder Wayland, 2001)
The Usborne World of Shakespeare by Anna Claybourne (Usborne, 2001)
What the Tudors and Stuarts Did for Us by Adam Hart-Davis (Boxtree, 2002)
Shakespeare and the Elizabethan Age by Andrew Langley (Treasure Chest, 2000)

Sightseers: Shakespeare's London (Kingfisher Books, 2002)
The Best Loved Plays of Shakespeare by Abigail Frost and Jennifer Mulherin (Cherrytree Books, 1997)
Shakespeare Stories (two volumes) by Leon Garfield (Puffin Books, 1997)
Shakespeare's Storybook by Patrick Ryan (Barefoot Books, 2001)

Video, DVD and CD-Rom

All Shakespeare's plays are available in several versions from the Royal Shakespeare Company and can be ordered from their website (see below)
Complete Works of Shakespeare on CD-Rom (Focus Multimedia)

Websites

www.springfield.k12.il.us/schools/springfield/eliz/elizabethanmedicine.html
http://elizabethan.org/compendium/index.html
www.tudorgroup.co.uk/articles/index.html
www.rcseng.ac.uk/about/history
www.rcplondon.ac.uk/heritage-centre/College-History/Pages/College-History.aspx
www.englishhistory.net/tudor.html
www.stratford.co.uk/shakespeare
www.rsc.org.uk
www.shakespeares-globe.org

Index